Tech Craft

Tracing the Development of Programming Languages

Texas Harmon

CONTENTS

Introduction

Tech Craft: The Development of Programming Languages

In the ever-evolving landscape of technology, programming languages stand as the foundational pillars, each telling a unique story of innovation, challenge, and progress. "Programming Languages: The Best" is a journey through the annals of computing history, exploring the origins, purposes, and legacies of some of the most influential programming languages that have shaped the digital world as we know it.

This book is not just a compilation of historical narratives; it is a tribute to the ingenuity and foresight of the individuals and teams who developed these languages. From the structured simplicity of COBOL in the 1950s to the modern versatility of Swift, each language has played a pivotal role in technological advancements and has left an indelible mark on the field of software development.

As you turn the pages, you will discover the stories behind languages like Java, which revolutionized web development with its "Write Once, Run Anywhere" philosophy, and JavaScript, which transformed the web from a static information medium into an interactive experience. You will delve into the origins of C and C++, languages that continue to be the bedrock of system-level programming, and PHP, a key player in the world of server-side scripting.

Our journey also includes insights into languages like R, which has become synonymous with statistical computing and data analysis, and TypeScript, which has enhanced

JavaScript with type safety and object-oriented features, reflecting the ever-growing complexity of web applications. We will also take a look at AI and briefly discuss it's role in the future of programming

This book is intended not just for programmers and computer science enthusiasts but for anyone curious about the evolution of digital languages and their impact on our lives. Whether you are a seasoned developer or new to the world of programming, "Tech Craft: The Development of Programming Languages" offers a comprehensive and accessible insight into the languages that have become the backbone of modern technology. This book also covers some popular markups and protocols.

As you embark on this enlightening exploration, we hope to increase your knowledge and awareness of these programming languages, not just as tools of technology, but as vibrant, evolving entities that continue to drive innovation and open new horizons in the realm of software development.

Welcome to a journey through the history, evolution, and enduring impact of the world's most significant programming languages.

Python

Introduction

Python, a high-level programming language known for its readability, simplicity, and broad applicability, has become a cornerstone in the world of software development. This article aims to provide a structured and detailed account of Python's creation, purpose, impact, and advancements over the years.

Creation

Python was conceived in the late 1980s by Guido van Rossum, a Dutch programmer, at Centrum Wiskunde & Informatica (CWI) in the Netherlands. The language was officially released in 1991 as Python 0.9.0. Van Rossum, influenced by his work on the ABC programming language, aimed to rectify ABC's shortcomings. Python was designed to be a highly readable language, with clear syntax and remarkable power. It was named after the British comedy series "Monty Python's Flying Circus," reflecting van Rossum's goal to create a language that was both powerful and fun to use.

Purpose and Design Philosophy

Python's primary objective was to support multiple programming paradigms, including procedural, object-oriented, and functional programming. The language emphasizes code readability and simplicity. Python's syntax allows programmers to express concepts in fewer lines of code than might be used in languages such as C++ or Java. The Python Enhancement Proposal (PEP) process, particularly PEP 20, known as "The Zen of Python," highlights these principles, stressing simplicity, readability, and the importance of good design.

Evolution and Impact

Python's evolution is marked by several significant milestones:

Python 2.0 (2000): Introduced list comprehensions, garbage collection, and Unicode support.

Python 3.0 (2008): A major revision designed to rectify fundamental design flaws, Python 3 was not completely backward-compatible with Python 2. Key features included improved consistency and the unification of text and data in Unicode.

Python's versatility in various fields, from web development to scientific computing, has cemented its status as one of the most popular programming languages. Its applications range from simple scripting to complex machine learning algorithms. The language's design and libraries have made it a favorite for data analysis, visualization, and artificial intelligence.

Community and Open-Source Development

Python's development is driven by an active community, which contributes to its extensive range of libraries and frameworks. The Python Software Foundation (PSF), a non-profit organization, oversees the development of Python. The open-source nature of Python means that it is freely available and modifiable, and has a large community of contributors.

Challenges and Criticisms

Despite its popularity, Python faces criticism for certain aspects, such as its execution speed. Python is often slower than compiled languages like C or Java. However, its ease of use and readability often outweigh these concerns, especially in data analysis and rapid prototyping.

Conclusion

Python's history reflects its status as a versatile and user-friendly language. Its continuous evolution, guided by its philosophy of simplicity and readability, has made it an invaluable tool in modern programming. As the landscape of technology shifts, Python adapts, maintaining its relevance and importance in the software development world.

COBOL - historically robust

Introduction

COBOL (Common Business-Oriented Language) emerged in the late 1950s as a groundbreaking programming language, designed to address the burgeoning needs of business data processing. It was created by a committee called CODASYL (Conference on Data Systems Languages), formed in response to the U.S. Department of Defense's desire for a standardized programming language that could run on different brands of computers. Grace Hopper, a pioneering computer scientist, played a crucial role in its development.

Purpose and Design

The language was intended to be readable and understandable by individuals who were not computer experts, mirroring English language constructs. This decision was revolutionary at the time and made COBOL highly accessible to a wider range of users. Its syntax, focusing on clarity and readability, made it particularly suited for business environments dealing with large amounts of data.

Impact and Legacy

COBOL quickly became a dominant force in the business computing sector. By the mid-1960s, it was one of the most widely used programming languages. Its design, which prioritized data processing and file handling, was perfectly suited for the era's typical business needs, such as payroll, inventory management, and other forms of record-keeping.

A significant portion of COBOL's legacy lies in its enduring use. As of the early 21st century, COBOL is still running significant portions of global financial systems, with billions of lines of code still in use. This longevity is a testament to its robustness and the foresight of its design.

Advancements and Evolution

Over the decades, COBOL has seen several versions and updates, adapting to new computing paradigms while maintaining its core principles. The language has been revised to include features such as object-orientation in later versions, a move that kept it relevant in a changing technological landscape.

Conclusion

COBOL stands as a monumental achievement in the history of programming languages. Its design philosophy, rooted in readability and practicality, set a precedent for future language development. Despite the evolution of technology, COBOL's legacy continues, underpinning critical systems in global finance and business, demonstrating the enduring value of well-designed technology solutions.

Java

Introduction

Java, a programming language and computing platform first released by Sun Microsystems in 1995, revolutionized the software industry. It was the brainchild of James Gosling and his team, known as the Green Team. They initiated the Java project to develop a language for digital devices such as set-top boxes, televisions, and others. However, the project pivoted to focus on the web, which was rapidly growing in popularity.

Purpose and Design

Java was designed to be a portable, high-performance language that could be used across various platforms, a concept encapsulated in its famous slogan, "Write Once, Run Anywhere." This cross-platform capability was facilitated through the Java Virtual Machine (JVM), which allows Java programs to run on any device equipped with a JVM.

Its syntax drew heavily from C and C++, making it familiar to a large pool of developers. Java's strong emphasis on reliability and robustness includes features like automatic memory management and strong typing, making it ideal for large-scale, complex applications.

Impact and Legacy

Java quickly became one of the world's most widely used programming languages, particularly favored for enterprise-level applications, Android mobile app development, and web applications. Its influence extended to the educational sector, where it has been a popular choice for teaching programming fundamentals.

Java's impact is also notable in its open-source ecosystem. The thriving community around Java has contributed to numerous frameworks, tools, and libraries, further cementing its place in the software development world.

Advancements and Evolution

Java has continually evolved, with regular updates adding new features and functionality. These updates have included enhancements for cloud computing, IoT applications, and performance improvements, ensuring Java's relevance in the fast-paced tech landscape.

Conclusion

Java represents a milestone in programming language design, emphasizing portability, performance, and versatility. Its enduring popularity and widespread use across various domains stand as a testament to its well-engineered design and the vision of its creators. Java continues to be a vital tool in modern software development, demonstrating adaptability and innovation in a rapidly evolving digital world.

JavaScript

Introduction

JavaScript, created by Brendan Eich in 1995 while working at Netscape Communications, rapidly evolved from a scripting tool for making web pages interactive to a fundamental technology of the World Wide Web. Initially developed under the name Mocha, then LiveScript, it was later renamed JavaScript to reflect Netscape's support of Java, though the two languages are distinct in design and function.

Purpose and Design

JavaScript was designed to enhance web pages by making them interactive and dynamic. It allows for client-side scripting, enabling web developers to add interactive elements to websites, which was a significant shift from the static web pages prevalent at that time.

The language is known for its flexibility and ease of use, making it accessible to a broad spectrum of developers, from beginners to experts. JavaScript supports multiple programming paradigms, including imperative, object-oriented, and functional programming, making it a versatile tool in the web development toolkit.

Impact and Legacy

JavaScript's impact on web development is monumental. It's an essential part of the trio of core technologies of the World Wide Web, alongside HTML and CSS. The introduction of AJAX (Asynchronous JavaScript and XML) in the early 2000s allowed web applications to send and retrieve data from a server asynchronously, enabling the creation of fast and dynamic web applications, a precursor to the modern web experience.

The emergence of Node.js in 2009 expanded JavaScript's reach beyond the browser, enabling server-side scripting and the development of scalable network applications. This has led to the full-stack development paradigm, where JavaScript can be used for both client-side and server-side programming.

Advancements and Evolution

JavaScript's ecosystem has seen rapid expansion with the introduction of numerous frameworks and libraries like React, Angular, and Vue.js, which have further simplified and enhanced web development practices.

The language itself has evolved, with ECMAScript (the standard that governs JavaScript) undergoing several revisions to add new features and improvements, ensuring that JavaScript stays current with the changing needs of web development.

Conclusion

JavaScript's role in shaping the modern web cannot be overstated. Its evolution from a simple scripting language to a powerful tool capable of creating complex, efficient, and interactive web applications marks it as a cornerstone of digital innovation. Its continued relevance in the tech industry is a testament to its adaptability and the vibrant community that supports and advances it.

C#

Introduction

C#, pronounced "C Sharp," is a modern, object-oriented programming language developed by Microsoft, led by Anders Hejlsberg. It was officially released in 2000 as part of Microsoft's .NET initiative. The language was conceived to combine the computing power of C++ with the programming ease of Visual Basic and has been integral to Microsoft's .NET framework.

Purpose and Design

C# was designed to be a versatile, safe, and developer-friendly language. It features strong typing, automatic memory management, and support for various programming paradigms, making it suitable for a wide range of applications, from web services to desktop applications.

The language's structure and syntax draw heavily from C and C++, but with several simplifications and improvements to reduce complexity and enhance readability. C# also incorporates elements from Java, making it familiar to a large number of developers.

Impact and Legacy

C#'s introduction played a significant role in the .NET framework, allowing developers to build robust and scalable applications across various platforms. Its tight integration with the .NET environment and Microsoft's backing has made it a popular choice for enterprise-level applications.

Over the years, C# has evolved significantly, keeping pace with new technological developments. Its use in developing Windows applications, web applications with ASP.NET, and even game development with the Unity game engine, demonstrates its versatility and broad appeal.

Advancements and Evolution

Microsoft has continually updated C# to include modern programming features such as asynchronous programming, LINQ (Language Integrated Query), and more. The introduction of .NET Core, a cross-platform version of .NET, has expanded C#'s reach, enabling the development of applications that run on Windows, Linux, and macOS.

The language has also embraced open-source development, with its compiler and core libraries available on GitHub, fostering a community-driven approach to its evolution.

Conclusion

C# is a testament to modern language design, successfully balancing power, flexibility, and developer productivity. Its ongoing development and adaptation to new computing paradigms ensure its continued relevance in the ever-changing landscape of software development.

C/C++

Introduction

C and C++ are two of the most fundamental programming languages in the history of computing. Developed in the early 1970s, C was created by Dennis Ritchie at Bell Labs. C++ was later developed by Bjarne Stroustrup in the early 1980s as an extension of C, hence the name "C++," which implies an increment of C.

Purpose and Design

C was designed for system programming and writing operating systems. Its low-level access to memory and simple set of keywords enabled efficient coding and provided direct control over hardware resources, which was essential in system development.

C++, on the other hand, introduced object-oriented features to C, making it suitable for large-scale software development. It provides the power of C with the added flexibility of classes, inheritance, polymorphism, and exception handling, among other features.

Impact and Legacy

The influence of C and C++ in the field of computer science and software development is profound. C was instrumental in the development of Unix and subsequently Linux, forming the backbone of many operating systems and embedded systems.

C++ enhanced the capabilities of C by introducing object-oriented programming (OOP) concepts, leading to its widespread adoption in software engineering, game development, and high-performance computing.

Advancements and Evolution

Both languages have evolved over the years. C remains popular due to its efficiency, portability, and role as a foundation for modern programming languages. It's still widely used in system programming, embedded systems, and other performance-critical applications.

C++ has undergone several standardizations, with the latest versions incorporating modern programming principles, greater abstraction capabilities, and increased performance and reliability.

Conclusion

C and C++ form the bedrock of modern software development, offering unparalleled control and efficiency. Their design principles and innovations have shaped the landscape of computing and continue to be vital in the development of high-performance and system-level applications.

PHP

Introduction

PHP, which stands for "PHP: Hypertext Preprocessor," is a widely-used open-source scripting language especially suited for web development. It was created by Rasmus Lerdorf in 1994 and has since become a fundamental tool in the creation of dynamic web content.

Purpose and Design

PHP was designed to enable the creation of dynamic web pages quickly and easily. It is a server-side scripting language, which means that PHP code is executed on the server, generating HTML which is then sent to the client's browser.

This approach allows for the creation of pages that can change or adjust content in response to user inputs, database interactions, or other factors.

The language is known for its simplicity and ease of use, which has contributed to its popularity among web developers. PHP integrates seamlessly with HTML and can be embedded directly into an HTML source document rather than requiring an external file for data processing.

Impact and Legacy

PHP played a significant role in shaping the modern web. It has been used to build some of the most popular websites and platforms on the internet, including WordPress, Facebook, and Wikipedia. Its ability to connect easily with MySQL, a popular database management system, has further solidified its position as a staple in web development.

PHP's widespread use can be attributed to its accessibility for beginners, extensive online community, and a rich ecosystem of frameworks and tools that simplify web development tasks.

Advancements and Evolution

Over the years, PHP has evolved, adding features and improvements to keep pace with the changing landscape of web development. The introduction of object-oriented programming features in PHP 5 and performance improvements in PHP 7 are among the notable advancements.

Conclusion

PHP remains a cornerstone of web development, known for its role in server-side scripting. Its enduring popularity is a testament to its adaptability, ease of use, and the rich functionality it brings to web development. PHP continues to be a go-to language for developers looking to build dynamic and interactive web applications.

Rust

Rust is a multi-paradigm programming language focused on performance, safety, and concurrency. It was first introduced by Graydon Hoare in 2006 as a personal project, and then sponsored by Mozilla Research. Rust has gained significant popularity and acclaim for its innovative approach to system-level programming, especially in areas where safety and performance are critical.

Inception and Design Philosophy

The development of Rust began with the aim to create a language that would overcome the pitfalls of existing languages used for system programming, particularly C and C++. Rust's design philosophy centers around three main goals: safety, speed, and concurrency.

One of Rust's primary innovations is its ownership model, which enforces memory safety without needing a garbage collector. This model enables Rust to prevent common programming bugs, like null pointer dereferencing and buffer overflows, at compile time, thereby enhancing the overall safety and security of the code.

Key Features and Advancements
Rust's most notable features include:

- **Ownership and Borrowing**: Unique features that manage memory and concurrency at compile time.
- **Zero-Cost Abstractions**: Rust provides abstractions that do not impose additional runtime overhead.
- **Fearless Concurrency**: Rust's ownership model naturally lends itself to writing safe concurrent code.
- **Memory Safety**: Rust enforces RAII (Resource Acquisition Is Initialization), ensuring safe memory management.
- **Cross-Platform**: Rust supports cross-platform development, running on multiple operating systems.
- **Cargo**: Rust's package manager and build system, simplifying dependency management and compilation.

Impact on Software Development
Rust is particularly known for its impact in areas where safety and performance are paramount, such as embedded systems, operating systems, and large-scale, high-performance services. Its memory safety guarantees and efficient concurrency model have made it a popular choice in these domains.

Additionally, Rust has been adopted by major tech companies for critical software infrastructure, further testifying to its reliability and robustness. The language has also fostered a vibrant open-source community, contributing to a wide range of projects.

Community and Ecosystem

The Rust community is known for its welcoming and inclusive nature. The Rust team places a strong emphasis on building a friendly and supportive environment, reflected in its comprehensive code of conduct. The community is actively involved in the development of the language, contributing to a rich ecosystem of libraries and tools.

Future Directions

Rust continues to evolve, with ongoing efforts to improve its compiler, enhance language features, and expand its standard library. The language is also seeing increased adoption in areas like WebAssembly, cloud computing, and more. As Rust matures, it is poised to redefine the landscape of system programming, setting new standards for performance, reliability, and safety in software development.

Conclusion

Rust represents a significant advancement in the field of programming languages. Its unique approach to memory safety, combined with its performance and concurrency features, positions it as a key player in modern software development. Rust's growing community and ecosystem are testaments to its potential to drive innovation in system-level programming for years to come.

R

Introduction

R is a programming language and software environment for statistical computing and graphics, developed by Ross Ihaka and Robert Gentleman at the University of Auckland, New Zealand, in the early 1990s. It has since become a cornerstone tool in data analysis, statistics, and graphical models.

Purpose and Design

The R language is designed primarily for statistical computing and data visualization. Its comprehensive array of statistical and graphical techniques, including linear and nonlinear modeling, classical statistical tests, time-series analysis, classification, and clustering, makes it a preferred choice among statisticians and data analysts.

R is an implementation of the S programming language combined with lexical scoping semantics inspired by Scheme. Its open-source nature and extensible features allow users to create custom functions and packages, further expanding its capabilities.

Impact and Legacy

R's impact in the fields of statistics and data science is substantial. It is widely used in academia and industry for data analysis, statistical modeling, and visualization. The language has fostered an active community of users who contribute to its extensive package ecosystem, making it adaptable to various data analysis tasks.

R's significance is also marked by its influence on the development of other programming languages and tools in data science, affirming its role as a pioneering tool in statistical computing.

Advancements and Evolution

R continues to evolve, with contributions from a global community of developers. This evolution includes improvements in performance, usability, and integration with other programming languages and tools. The language is also adapting to modern data science needs, including big data analytics and machine learning.

Conclusion

R remains a fundamental tool in the toolkit of statisticians and data scientists, celebrated for its versatility in data analysis and graphical capabilities. Its enduring popularity and ongoing development reflect its adaptability and importance in the rapidly evolving field of data science.

TypeScript

Introduction

TypeScript is an open-source programming language developed and maintained by Microsoft. It was first introduced in 2012 as a superset of JavaScript, designed to add static typing to the language. TypeScript was created by Anders Hejlsberg, the lead architect of C# and creator of Delphi and Turbo Pascal.

Purpose and Design

The primary goal of TypeScript is to improve the development experience for applications written in

JavaScript, particularly those of a larger scale. TypeScript adds optional static typing to JavaScript, which can help catch errors early through a type system and provide better tooling support for autocompletion, navigation, and refactoring.

TypeScript is designed to be compiled to clean, simple JavaScript code which runs on any browser, in Node.js, or in any JavaScript engine that supports ECMAScript 3 (or newer). This makes TypeScript highly versatile and compatible with existing JavaScript codebases.

Impact and Legacy

TypeScript has significantly influenced web development, particularly in complex projects where JavaScript's dynamic typing can become challenging to manage. It offers a solution that scales well for large codebases and teams, improving maintainability and developer productivity.

The language has been widely adopted in the web development community, with many popular frameworks and libraries offering TypeScript support or being rewritten in TypeScript to enhance their robustness and usability.

Advancements and Evolution

TypeScript continues to evolve, with frequent updates that introduce improvements in typing, tooling, and compatibility with modern JavaScript features. The TypeScript team actively engages with the community to incorporate feedback and ensure the language meets the needs of modern web development.

Conclusion

TypeScript represents a significant advancement in web development, offering a powerful tool for building more reliable and maintainable JavaScript applications. Its growing popularity and continuous development reflect its value in the rapidly evolving landscape of web technologies.

Swift

Introduction

Swift is a powerful and intuitive programming language created by Apple Inc. for building apps for iOS, macOS, watchOS, and tvOS. First introduced at Apple's Worldwide Developers Conference in 2014, Swift was designed to be a more approachable and safer alternative to Objective-C, the then-standard for Apple app development.

Purpose and Design

Swift was designed with a focus on performance, safety, and expressiveness. It incorporates modern language features like closures, generics, and type inference, making code more concise and readable. Swift's syntax and design encourage developers to write clean and consistent code that is less prone to errors.

One of the key features of Swift is its safety. The language is designed to eliminate entire categories of common programming errors by adopting modern programming patterns and strong typing. This makes Swift applications less prone to bugs and crashes.

Impact and Legacy

Swift has rapidly gained popularity among developers for its efficiency and ease of use. It has significantly influenced the development of iOS and macOS applications, allowing for the creation of more reliable and performant applications. Swift's impact extends beyond Apple's ecosystem, as it has fostered a vibrant community of developers and contributed to the advancement of mobile app development.

Advancements and Evolution

Swift continues to evolve with regular updates that enhance its capabilities and introduce new features. Apple's commitment to Swift's development is evident in its open-source nature, allowing the broader developer community to contribute to its growth and adaptation.

Conclusion

Swift represents a significant step forward in the field of mobile application development. Its emphasis on safety, performance, and readability makes it an ideal choice for modern app development, and its ongoing evolution ensures it remains at the forefront of technological innovation.

Objective-C

Introduction

Objective-C is a programming language that was essential in the development of Apple's iOS and macOS operating systems. It was originally developed in the early 1980s by Brad Cox and Tom Love at their company, StepStone. Objective-C was later adopted by Apple in the late 1980s and became the backbone of Apple's software development for decades.

Purpose and Design

Objective-C was an extension of the C programming language, incorporating object-oriented capabilities and dynamic runtime. It was designed to offer a powerful object-oriented programming environment but with minimal language extensions. The language is known for its unique syntax, which blends C-style syntax with Smalltalk-style messaging.

The language was primarily used for Apple's iOS and macOS applications, providing the foundation for the development of many of the early and iconic Apple applications and technologies.

Impact and Legacy

Objective-C played a significant role in the development of Apple's software ecosystem. It was the main programming language used for macOS (originally NeXTSTEP) and later iOS until the introduction of Swift. Objective-C's dynamic runtime made it particularly well-suited for the rapid development of graphical user interfaces and applications for Apple devices.

Despite being largely superseded by Swift in recent years, Objective-C's legacy persists in the vast number of existing applications and libraries written in the language. It remains an important part of the Apple development ecosystem, particularly for maintaining and updating legacy code.

Advancements and Evolution

Over the years, Objective-C underwent various enhancements to keep up with the evolving needs of Apple's software development. This includes improvements in memory management, the introduction of blocks (closures), and the integration with Apple's Cocoa and Cocoa Touch frameworks.

Conclusion

Objective-C's contribution to the world of software development, particularly in the context of Apple's ecosystem, is undeniable. Its unique blend of C and object-oriented programming influenced a generation of Apple software and paved the way for the modern development landscape represented by Swift.

SQL

SQL, or Structured Query Language, is a domain-specific language used in programming and designed for managing data held in a relational database management system (RDBMS), or for stream processing in a relational data stream management system (RDSMS). It is particularly effective in handling structured data, i.e., data incorporating relations among entities and variables.

Inception

SQL was developed at IBM by Donald D. Chamberlin and Raymond F. Boyce in the early 1970s. It was originally known as SEQUEL (Structured English Query Language) and was designed to manipulate and retrieve data stored in IBM's original quasi-relational database management system, System R. The acronym SEQUEL was later shortened to SQL due to trademark issues.

Purpose and Design

The primary function of SQL is to query data from a database. It offers a range of operations for data insertion, query, update, and delete, as well as schema creation and modification, and data access control. SQL's design follows a declarative programming style, meaning that the language specifies what needs to be done rather than how to do it.

Impact and Advancements

SQL significantly transformed database management. By the late 1980s, it had become the standard database language, largely due to its adoption by ANSI (American National Standards Institute) in 1986 and subsequently by the International Organization for Standardization (ISO) in 1987. Since then, SQL has undergone several enhancements, including the addition of features for procedural programming, triggers, and support for object-oriented programming concepts. These advancements have made SQL integral to the fields of data science, online transaction processing, and data warehousing.

Continued Relevance

Today, SQL remains a cornerstone of database management. Its use extends across various database systems like MySQL, PostgreSQL, and Microsoft SQL Server. The language's ability to handle large-scale data efficiently and its integration with other technologies, such as big data and cloud computing, underscore its ongoing relevance in the rapidly evolving domain of data management and analytics.

The evolution of SQL is a testament to its robust design and adaptability, marking it as a pivotal technology in the realm of data handling and analysis.

Evolution and Standardization

The evolution of SQL has been marked by a series of standardizations and enhancements, reflecting its growing importance in data management. The first standard, SQL-86 or SQL-87, established the foundational aspects of the language. Subsequent revisions, including SQL-92, SQL:1999, SQL:2003, and SQL:2011, introduced significant new features like support for recursive queries, triggers, standardized sequences, and common table expressions.

These standardizations have ensured that SQL evolves in a consistent and interoperable manner, allowing different database systems to adopt a core set of features. This interoperability is crucial in a world where data is often distributed across various systems and needs to be accessed and manipulated in a standardized way.

SQL in Modern Computing

In the context of modern computing, SQL plays a critical role in both traditional and innovative applications. With the advent of big data technologies, SQL has been adapted to work with non-relational databases as well, leading to the development of NoSQL (Not Only SQL) databases, which offer greater scalability and flexibility for certain types of data and queries.

Additionally, SQL interfaces are commonly used in business intelligence applications, enabling non-technical users to interact with complex data through more accessible front-end tools. This democratization of data access and manipulation has been a significant driver in the field of data analytics and business decision-making.

Challenges and Adaptations

Despite its widespread use, SQL faces challenges, particularly in handling unstructured data and in environments where the scale of data is massive, such as in big data applications. In response, there have been adaptations in SQL, including the development of extensions and variations like T-SQL (Transact-SQL) and PL/SQL (Procedural Language/SQL), which add procedural programming elements to the standard SQL.

Furthermore, the integration of SQL with other programming paradigms and its extension to support JSON and XML data formats show the language's adaptability to the changing needs of the data management landscape.

Conclusion

SQL's journey from a database querying language to a multifaceted tool integral to data management underscores its importance in the computing world. Its ability to evolve, adapt to new technologies, and maintain standardization has established SQL as a timeless tool in the programmer's toolkit. As data continues to be a pivotal aspect of modern computing, SQL's role in efficiently managing, querying, and analyzing this data ensures its continued relevance in the future of technology.

CSS

Cascading Style Sheets (CSS) is a style sheet language used for describing the presentation of a document written in a markup language like HTML. CSS is a cornerstone technology of the World Wide Web, alongside HTML and JavaScript.

Inception

CSS was first proposed by Håkon Wium Lie on October 10, 1994. At the time, the web was growing rapidly, but there was a clear need for style sheets to manage the appearance of web pages. The proposal for CSS was made to the World Wide Web Consortium (W3C), the main international standards organization for the World Wide Web.

Purpose and Design

The primary purpose of CSS is to enable the separation of presentation and content, including layout, colors, and fonts. This separation improves content accessibility, provides more flexibility and control in the specification of presentation characteristics, and reduces complexity and repetition in the structural content.

CSS uses a series of rules or directives to define how a given element or group of elements should be displayed. A CSS rule consists of a selector and a declaration block. The selector points to the HTML element to style, and the declaration block contains one or more declarations separated by semicolons. Each declaration includes a CSS property name and a value, separated by a colon.

Impact and Advancements

CSS has had a profound impact on web design and development. Before its introduction, styling web pages was cumbersome, often requiring inline styles or complex scripting. CSS introduced a more streamlined and efficient method for styling, dramatically changing the way websites are designed and built.

Over the years, CSS has evolved through several versions, with CSS1, CSS2, and CSS3 being the most notable. CSS3, in particular, introduced a wide range of new features like animations, transitions, gradients, and grid layouts, enabling more sophisticated and interactive web designs.

Challenges and Adaptations

One of the primary challenges in CSS has been browser compatibility, with different browsers interpreting CSS rules in slightly different ways. This has led to the need for browser-specific prefixes and workarounds in CSS code. However, the situation has improved significantly with the standardization efforts by W3C and better adherence to standards by browser developers.

Moreover, the rise of mobile internet usage has introduced new challenges in responsive design, leading to CSS extensions like Flexbox and CSS Grid Layout, which provide more robust tools for creating responsive and adaptable web layouts.

Conclusion

CSS continues to be an essential tool in web development, offering unparalleled control over the visual presentation of web content. Its evolution from a simple style sheet mechanism to a powerful tool for creating responsive, interactive web designs reflects its critical role in shaping the appearance of the World Wide Web. As web technologies continue to evolve, CSS is likely to remain a key player in defining how content is presented across diverse platforms and devices.

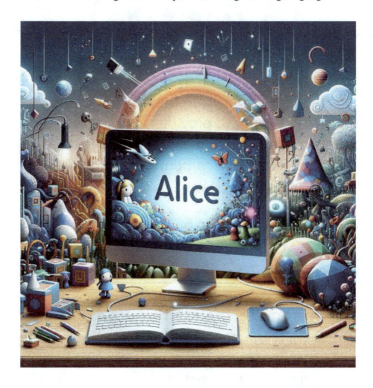

Alice

Alice is an innovative block-based programming language that makes it easy to create animations, build interactive narratives, or program simple games in 3D. Developed primarily as an educational tool, Alice introduces students to fundamental programming concepts in an engaging and less intimidating environment.

Inception

Alice was developed by Randy Pausch and his team at Carnegie Mellon University in the late 1990s. The project was born out of the desire to provide a more accessible introduction to programming, particularly for students without a background in computer science. The name "Alice" was chosen in honor of Lewis Carroll's character Alice from "Alice in Wonderland," symbolizing an adventure into the new and unexplored world of programming.

Purpose and Design

Alice's primary goal is to teach logical and computational thinking skills, fundamental principles of programming, and basic object-oriented programming concepts in a visual and narrative-driven environment. Its user-friendly interface allows students to drag and drop graphic tiles to create a program, where each tile represents a logical structure or a programming function. This approach reduces the intimidation and frustration often associated with syntax errors in traditional text-based programming.

Impact and Advancements

Alice has significantly impacted computer science education by providing an accessible and engaging platform for introductory programming. It has been widely adopted in schools around the world and has inspired a generation of students to explore computer science. Alice's approach to teaching through storytelling and game-like experiences has influenced other educational programming languages and tools.

Furthermore, Alice has evolved to support various features like object manipulation, event handling, and scenario-based learning, making it a versatile tool for teaching different aspects of programming in a visually rich 3D environment.

Challenges and Adaptations

Despite its effectiveness as an educational tool, Alice faces challenges in bridging the gap between block-based programming and more advanced text-based programming languages. To address this, educators often use Alice as a stepping stone, introducing students to programming concepts in a friendly environment before transitioning them to more traditional languages.

Additionally, Alice continues to adapt and evolve, with newer versions expanding its capabilities, improving its user interface, and providing more resources for educators and learners.

Conclusion

Alice stands as a pioneering tool in computer science education, breaking down barriers to learning programming and making it accessible to a wider audience. Its innovative use of storytelling, drag-and-drop programming, and a visually rich 3D environment has made it an influential model in educational technology. As computer science education continues to evolve, Alice's legacy as a tool that makes learning programming fun and engaging will continue to inspire future educational innovations.

NoSQL

NoSQL, an acronym for "Not Only SQL," represents a shift from traditional relational database management systems (RDBMS) towards more flexible and scalable systems for handling data. This change in data management philosophy arose primarily to address the limitations of SQL databases, especially when dealing with large volumes of unstructured or semi-structured data.

Inception and Evolution

The term "NoSQL" was first used in 1998 by Carlo Strozzi to describe his lightweight, file-based database which did not expose a SQL interface. However, the concept gained significant momentum in the late 2000s, when the increasing demands of web-scale applications necessitated databases that could scale horizontally and handle unstructured data efficiently. Companies like Google and Amazon were among the pioneers in this field, developing their own NoSQL systems (Bigtable and DynamoDB, respectively) to meet their unique data storage and retrieval challenges.

Purpose and Characteristics

NoSQL databases are characterized by their non-reliance on a fixed schema, unlike traditional RDBMS which use a structured query language (SQL) and have a predefined schema. This flexibility allows NoSQL databases to store and manage various data types, including documents, key-value pairs, wide-column stores, and graph databases. They are particularly adept at handling large volumes of data and high user loads, which make them ideal for big data applications, real-time web applications, and distributed computing.

Types of NoSQL Databases

- **Document Databases**: Store data in document-like structures (e.g., JSON, BSON). Examples include MongoDB and Couchbase.
- **Key-Value Stores**: The simplest form of NoSQL databases, storing data as a collection of key-value pairs. Redis and DynamoDB are notable examples.
- **Wide-Column Stores**: Optimize for queries over large datasets, storing data in columns rather than rows. Examples are Cassandra and HBase.
- **Graph Databases**: Designed for data whose relationships are best represented as a graph. Neo4j and Amazon Neptune are examples.

Impact and Advancements

NoSQL databases have significantly impacted how data is stored and retrieved, particularly in environments where data variety, volume, and velocity are critical factors. They have enabled the development of flexible and scalable applications, crucial for modern web and cloud services. Technological advancements in NoSQL databases continue to evolve, focusing on improved query capabilities, enhanced consistency models, and seamless integration with other data platforms.

The adoption of NoSQL technologies has also influenced the development of new data processing frameworks and paradigms, such as MapReduce and streaming data processing, further expanding the possibilities in the field of big data and real-time analytics.

In conclusion, NoSQL databases have emerged as vital tools in the data management landscape, offering alternatives to traditional SQL databases where flexibility, scalability, and performance are paramount. As data continues to grow in size and complexity, NoSQL technologies are likely to play an increasingly significant role in addressing the evolving needs of modern computing.

Challenges and Considerations

While NoSQL databases offer numerous advantages, they also present unique challenges and considerations. One of the primary challenges is ensuring data consistency, especially in distributed systems where data is replicated across multiple nodes. Unlike SQL databases that typically follow the ACID (Atomicity, Consistency, Isolation, Durability) properties, NoSQL databases often employ eventual consistency to achieve higher performance and availability, which may not be suitable for all applications.

Another consideration is the learning curve associated with NoSQL databases. Each type of NoSQL database (document, key-value, wide-column, graph) has its own model and query language, which can be quite different from traditional SQL. This diversity requires developers and database administrators to learn and adapt to different systems depending on their specific use cases.

Integration with Existing Systems

Integrating NoSQL databases into existing systems, which are often built around relational databases, poses its own set of challenges. Ensuring compatibility and efficient data transfer between SQL and NoSQL systems requires careful planning and execution. Moreover, organizations often need to maintain a balance between leveraging the strengths of NoSQL for certain applications while continuing to utilize their existing SQL databases for others.

Future Directions

The future of NoSQL is likely to see continued growth and evolution. One area of development is in enhancing the querying and analytics capabilities of NoSQL databases, bridging the gap between the flexibility of NoSQL and the robust querying features of SQL databases. Another area is the further integration of NoSQL databases with machine learning and artificial intelligence applications, where their ability to handle large, diverse datasets can be particularly advantageous.

Conclusion

NoSQL databases represent a paradigm shift in data management, offering scalable, flexible solutions for modern data needs. While they are not a one-size-fits-all solution and come with their own set of challenges, their impact on the landscape of data storage and retrieval is undeniable. As the digital world continues to evolve and generate vast amounts of data, NoSQL technologies will remain key players in managing, processing, and deriving value from this data.

HTML

Introduction

HTML, short for HyperText Markup Language, stands as the foundational language of the World Wide Web. Developed as a means to create structured documents for the internet, HTML has evolved from a simple markup language to a pivotal tool in web development and design.

Historical Context

The inception of HTML dates back to 1989 when Tim Berners-Lee, a British computer scientist at CERN, proposed a new system for sharing documents. This system, which later became known as the World Wide Web, needed a simple language to structure and link documents - thus, HTML was born. The first documented version of HTML was in 1991, featuring a handful of basic tags that were sufficient for basic web page construction.

Evolution and Standardization

HTML's evolution is a testament to the rapid development of web technologies. The early 90s saw the introduction of new tags and attributes in quick succession, albeit in an unstandardized format. This period was marked by browser wars, where different web browsers supported different versions of HTML.

The formation of the World Wide Web Consortium (W3C) in 1994 brought much-needed standardization. HTML 2.0, released in 1995, became the first standard, setting a baseline for future developments. HTML 4.01, a significant update, introduced features like frames and scripts, which were revolutionary at the time.

The most transformative update came with HTML5, introduced in 2014. This version integrated multimedia capabilities natively, eliminating the need for third-party plugins. It also introduced semantic elements, improving web accessibility and SEO.

HTML's Impact

HTML's impact on the digital world is immeasurable. It has democratized information, enabling individuals and organizations to publish content globally. Its simplicity allows people with minimal technical knowledge to create web pages, contributing to an ever-expanding internet.

Moreover, HTML has been a catalyst for advancements in web technologies. It laid the groundwork for cascading style sheets (CSS) and JavaScript, which together with HTML form the core triad of web development.

Current State and Future Directions

Today, HTML continues to evolve. The focus has shifted towards making the web more accessible and performant. Features like Web Components and improvements in semantic markup are steps in this direction.

The future of HTML is likely to be shaped by emerging web technologies like augmented reality (AR), virtual reality (VR), and the Internet of Things (IoT). As these technologies mature, HTML will adapt to accommodate new types of content and interaction paradigms.

Conclusion

HTML's journey from a simple document structuring tool to the backbone of the digital age is a story of technological triumph. Its ongoing evolution and adaptation reflect the dynamic nature of the web and its central role in the digital ecosystem. As the internet continues to evolve, so will HTML, adapting to new challenges and shaping the future of digital content.

Visual Basic

Introduction

Visual Basic, often abbreviated as VB, is an event-driven programming language from Microsoft that is known for its Component Object Model (COM) programming model. First released in 1991, it was designed to be easy to learn and use, making it particularly popular among beginners.

Historical Context

The origins of Visual Basic date back to the earlier BASIC language, developed in the 1960s. BASIC was created to enable students to write programs using time-shared computers. With the advent of the personal computer, Microsoft saw an opportunity to create a graphical version of BASIC, leading to the development of Visual Basic.

Development and Features

Visual Basic was revolutionary because it allowed developers to create Windows applications easily. Its drag-and-drop interface for creating user interfaces, combined with its simplified code structure, lowered the barrier to entry for Windows programming.

One of the key features of Visual Basic was its Integrated Development Environment (IDE), which included tools for designing user interfaces and debugging code. It introduced concepts like "forms" (for designing GUIs) and "controls" (like buttons and text boxes), which could be easily manipulated in the IDE.

Impact and Legacy

The impact of Visual Basic was significant in making programming more accessible. Its simplicity attracted a new generation of developers, and it played a critical role in the proliferation of custom business applications during the 1990s and early 2000s.

Visual Basic also influenced the development of .NET, Microsoft's framework for building applications across web, mobile, and desktop platforms. Visual Basic .NET, an updated version compatible with the .NET framework, introduced object-oriented programming features, broadening its scope and utility.

Current State and Outlook

While the original version of Visual Basic is no longer in active development, Visual Basic .NET continues to be a vital part of the .NET ecosystem. Its current role is more specialized, often used in business environments for developing internal applications.

The future of Visual Basic .NET is tied to the evolution of the .NET framework. As Microsoft continues to invest in .NET, Visual Basic .NET will likely remain a relevant option for enterprise application development, especially for those already invested in the Microsoft ecosystem.

Conclusion

Visual Basic's legacy as a pioneering tool in simplifying Windows application development is undeniable. It democratized programming by making it more accessible and laid the foundation for the more advanced and versatile Visual Basic .NET. As the technological landscape evolves, Visual Basic remains an important chapter in the history of programming languages.

Ruby

Ruby is a dynamic, open-source programming language with a focus on simplicity and productivity. It has an elegant syntax that is natural to read and easy to write. Created by Yukihiro "Matz" Matsumoto in Japan in the mid-1990s, Ruby combines parts of his favorite languages (Perl, Smalltalk, Eiffel, Ada, and Lisp) to form a new language that balanced functional programming with imperative programming.

Inception and Philosophy

The development of Ruby began in 1993, with the first public release, Ruby 0.95, released in 1995. Matsumoto sought to create a new language that emphasized human needs over those of the computer, following the principle of least surprise (POLS), where the language would behave in a way that minimizes confusion for experienced users.

Matsumoto has often said that he is "trying to make Ruby natural, not simple," reflecting a philosophy that emphasizes human-centric design over machine-centric. This approach is evident in Ruby's syntax, which is often described as almost reading like English, which makes it both easy to use for beginners and powerful for experienced programmers.

Key Features

Ruby's key features include an object-oriented architecture, support for multiple programming paradigms, and a dynamic type system. It also offers memory management, which is facilitated by a garbage collector. Ruby's syntax is designed to be intuitive and its operations straightforward, which has led to its description as a "programmer's best friend."

Notable aspects of Ruby include:

- **Object-Oriented**: Everything in Ruby is an object, including primitive data types.
- **Flexible**: Ruby allows users to freely alter its parts. Essential elements of the language can be removed or redefined, at the risk of making the program less readable.
- **Mixin Modules**: Rather than using multiple inheritances, Ruby offers mixins as a better way to share functionality between classes.
- **Block Usage**: Ruby blocks are anonymous functions that can be passed into methods. They are a fundamental and powerful feature of Ruby.

Impact and Advancements

Ruby gained popularity with the release of Ruby on Rails in 2004, a full-stack web framework that made it easy to build powerful web applications. The philosophy of Rails, convention over configuration, further emphasized Ruby's principle of making programming more about human needs than computer needs.

Ruby has significantly influenced various programming languages, such as Elixir, and has been used for desktop applications, servers, and in various frameworks and libraries. Its ease of use and productivity benefits have made it a popular choice for startups and established companies alike.

The language continues to evolve, with regular updates and a strong community supporting its growth and refinement. Ruby is known for its culture of testing and has a rich set of tools and frameworks that support test-driven development (TDD).

Ruby demonstrates a unique blend of simplicity, elegance, and power, making it a distinctive and beloved language in the programming community.

Community and Ecosystem

Ruby's community is one of its greatest strengths. The language has fostered an inclusive and supportive culture, which is evident in the numerous conferences, meet-ups, and online forums dedicated to Ruby development. Rubyists, as Ruby programmers are affectionately known, often emphasize the importance of "Matz is nice, so we are nice"

(MINASWAN), a motto that captures the community's spirit of friendliness and collaboration.

The Ruby ecosystem is rich with libraries, known as "gems," which provide additional functionality. RubyGems, the Ruby package manager, simplifies the process of distributing and installing these libraries. The availability of a wide range of gems enables developers to build applications quickly and efficiently by leveraging existing solutions for common problems.

Challenges and Criticism

Despite its many strengths, Ruby faces challenges and criticism, particularly regarding performance. Ruby's runtime speed has been a point of contention, especially when compared to languages like Java or C++. However, successive versions of Ruby have made significant improvements in performance, with the introduction of features like Just-In-Time (JIT) compilation in recent versions.

Scalability has also been a subject of debate in the Ruby community. While Ruby on Rails applications can scale effectively, they often require careful planning and optimization. This challenge is not unique to Ruby, but it is a consideration for developers building large-scale applications.

Future Prospects

The future of Ruby is closely tied to ongoing developments in web technology and the evolving needs of programmers. With a strong community and a culture of innovation, Ruby is likely to continue adapting and evolving. The introduction of new features and performance enhancements, along with Ruby's inherent strengths in rapid application development and ease of use, position it well for continued relevance in the programming landscape.

Ruby's philosophy of prioritizing developer happiness and productivity remains a guiding principle. As technology evolves, Ruby's adaptability and the commitment of its community suggest that it will continue to be a prominent and cherished tool in the programmer's toolkit.

Ruby represents a significant achievement in the field of programming languages, combining technical sophistication with a unique emphasis on human-centric design. Its continued evolution and the passionate community that surrounds it are testaments to its enduring appeal and effectiveness as a programming tool.

Educational Impact

Ruby has also made a considerable impact in the realm of education. Its simple and readable syntax makes it an excellent language for teaching programming concepts to beginners. Educational tools and programs often choose Ruby as a starting point for teaching object-oriented programming, demonstrating basic programming constructs, and introducing web development.

Universities, coding bootcamps, and online courses frequently feature Ruby in their curricula, valuing its balance between simplicity and real-world applicability. This educational presence not only helps in nurturing new programmers but also contributes to a constant influx of talent into the Ruby community.

Integration and Compatibility

Ruby's ability to interface with other programming languages and technologies is another notable aspect. It can be embedded into web applications, run on virtual machines, and interface with various database systems. Ruby's interoperability with front-end technologies and frameworks allows for full-stack development capabilities, making it a versatile choice for a wide range of projects.

Furthermore, Ruby's compatibility with major operating systems, including Linux, macOS, and Windows, ensures its accessibility to a broad audience of developers. This cross-platform compatibility is crucial for developing applications that need to run in diverse environments.

Contribution to Open Source

Ruby's significance extends to its contribution to open source software. Being open-source itself, Ruby encourages a culture of open collaboration and sharing. Numerous Ruby-based projects have significantly influenced the open-source landscape, fostering innovation and community-driven development.

The open-source nature of Ruby and its libraries allows developers to contribute to its development, propose changes, and fix bugs, making it a collective effort of the global developer community. This participatory approach has led to a robust, flexible, and continuously improving language ecosystem.

Conclusion

In conclusion, Ruby is more than just a programming language; it's a community, a philosophy, and a tool that empowers developers to create with ease and joy. Its influence on programming, web development, education, and open-source software is profound. As it continues to evolve, Ruby remains a testament to the beauty and power of well-crafted technology, designed with both the developer and the end user in mind. Its legacy lies in its ability to simplify complex problems, foster a supportive community, and continually adapt to the changing landscape of technology.

Artificial Intelligence (AI)

Artificial Intelligence (AI) is a field of computer science that aims to create machines capable of intelligent behavior. Pioneered in the mid-20th century, AI has evolved from theoretical research into a diverse array of technologies that are transforming multiple aspects of our lives. From machine learning algorithms to intelligent robotics, AI is rapidly reshaping the technological landscape.

Inception and Philosophical Foundations

AI's roots can be traced back to the ancient Greek myths of intelligent robots and automatons. Modern AI began with classical philosophers' attempts to describe human thinking as a symbolic system, leading to the invention of programmable digital computers, a necessary precondition for AI.

In 1956, the term "Artificial Intelligence" was coined at the Dartmouth Conference, which is often considered the birth of AI as an independent field. Early AI research in the 1950s and 1960s focused on symbolic methods and problem-solving, including areas like logic and reasoning, knowledge representation, and learning from data.

Key Developments and Technologies

AI encompasses various subfields, each with unique methodologies and applications:

- **Machine Learning**: Enables computers to learn from data and make decisions or predictions.
- **Natural Language Processing (NLP)**: Focuses on enabling computers to understand, interpret, and respond to human language.
- **Robotics**: Involves the creation of robots that can perform tasks autonomously.
- **Computer Vision**: Gives machines the ability to understand and interpret visual information from the world.
- **Expert Systems**: Designed to mimic the decision-making ability of a human expert.

Deep learning, a subset of machine learning involving neural networks with many layers, has been instrumental in recent advances in AI, particularly in fields like image and speech recognition.

Impact on Society and Industry

AI's impact is vast and growing. It has transformed industries by optimizing processes, enhancing data analytics, and creating new ways of interacting with technology. In healthcare, AI assists in diagnosis and personalized medicine. In finance, it's used for risk assessment and fraud detection. In transportation, AI powers self-driving vehicles and smart traffic management systems.

The integration of AI into everyday life has raised important questions about privacy, ethics, and the future of work. As AI systems become more sophisticated, ensuring they are fair, transparent, and aligned with human values is a growing concern.

Future Prospects and Challenges

AI's future is both promising and challenging. Continued advancements in computational power and algorithms will likely lead to more sophisticated and autonomous AI systems. However, challenges such as bias in AI algorithms, the potential for job displacement, and the ethical implications of autonomous decision-making remain significant issues that need to be addressed.

The development of explainable AI, which aims to make AI decision-making processes transparent and understandable, is a crucial area of ongoing research. Similarly, the pursuit of artificial general intelligence (AGI) – AI that can understand, learn, and apply its intelligence broadly like a human – remains a long-term goal.

Conclusion

Artificial Intelligence represents a pinnacle of human ingenuity, reflecting our quest to understand and replicate our cognitive abilities. Its development has not only opened up new technological possibilities but also posed new ethical and philosophical questions. As AI continues to evolve, it will undoubtedly play an increasingly central role in shaping the future of humanity.

The Role of AI in Programming Languages

The integration of Artificial Intelligence (AI) into programming languages represents a significant leap in the field of software development. AI's role in programming encompasses various dimensions, from automating mundane coding tasks to revolutionizing how we approach problem-solving in software development.

Enhancing Coding Efficiency

One of the primary roles of AI in programming languages is to enhance the efficiency of coding. Tools powered by AI can assist in writing code, detecting bugs, and suggesting optimizations. Integrated Development Environments (IDEs) equipped with AI capabilities can offer real-time feedback, code completion, and intelligent refactoring suggestions. This not only speeds up the development process but also helps in maintaining the quality and consistency of the code.

AI-Powered Code Analysis

AI algorithms are increasingly being used for code analysis. By learning from vast repositories of existing code, AI can identify patterns and anomalies that might be missed by human programmers. This capability is particularly useful in identifying potential security vulnerabilities and performance bottlenecks. Such analysis not only improves the security and efficiency of software but also serves as a learning tool for developers.

Facilitating Language Translations

AI plays a pivotal role in translating code between different programming languages. Through advanced machine learning models, AI can understand the semantics of one language and replicate its functionality in another. This capacity is invaluable in modern software development environments where systems are often built using multiple programming languages.

Personalized Learning and Adaptation

AI in programming languages is not just about automation; it's also about personalization. AI systems can adapt to a programmer's style and preferences, providing customized suggestions and learning resources. This personalized approach helps in accelerating the learning curve for new programmers and enhancing the productivity of experienced developers.

Predictive Programming and Auto-Generation of Code

Emerging AI technologies are moving towards predictive programming and auto-generation of code. AI systems are being trained to predict what a programmer intends to write next, offering suggestions to complete code blocks. In some cases, AI can auto-generate entire segments of code based on high-level requirements, significantly reducing the manual coding effort.

Challenges and Ethical Considerations

The integration of AI into programming raises several challenges and ethical considerations. Dependence on AI tools for coding might lead to a decrease in fundamental programming skills among new developers. There is also the challenge of ensuring that AI-generated code is reliable, secure, and free from biases inherent in the training data.

Conclusion

The role of AI in programming languages is transformative, offering unprecedented efficiencies and capabilities. It is reshaping the landscape of software development, making it more efficient, accessible, and innovative. As AI technology continues to evolve, its integration with programming languages is expected to deepen, leading to more intelligent, adaptive, and efficient software development processes.

ABOUT THE AUTHOR

Texas Harmon is a hobby researcher, writer, and developer with an interest in how technology shapes our world and the use of technology to enhance communication and creativity.

www.ingramcontent.com/pod-product-compliance
Lightning Source LLC
La Vergne TN
LVHW051644050326
832903LV00022B/879